BACK YOURSELF

Don't Give Up When You Have to Step Up

By Rinus Le Roux

PUBLISHING AND COPYRIGHT

BACK YOURSELF, By Rinus Le Roux

Print ISBN 9780620589246, eBook ISBN 9781365610714

Published by The UCan Institute, P O Box 527, Parklands, 2121, Johannesburg, Gauteng

Printed and bound: Conti Print, P O Box 30990, Braamfontein, 2017, Tel: 011 334 1484

Creative direction, Rehann Calitz - calitz.rehann@iburst.co.za

Illustration: Sandile Radebe - 0797325823

Design and layout, Lisa Borman - 082 990 2938

Editing and proof reading, Valda Strauss - 082 686 4483

Cover photograph, Channay Harvey

Layout, eBook conversion and online distribution by www.bulabuka.co.za

CONTENTS

ABOUT THE AUTHOR

Rinus le Roux is a professional speaker, trainer and author.

His life is dedicated to the development of human potential.

He observes, contemplates and comments on human behaviour and how to improve it.

rinus@ucan.co.za

www.ucan.co.za

DEDICATION

This book is dedicated to Hanlie (Bella).

To me you are the ultimate example of what it means to back yourself in every way possible.

You inspire me and for that I serve you.

ACKNOWLEDGEMENT

In the absence of that which I am not, that which I am cannot exist. Neale Donald Walsch

Thank you for being who you are so that I can be who I am.

INTRODUCTION

It's break time on an ordinary school day. I am in Grade 10 (Std 8) and am trying to find a place where Albert, the Grade 12 (matric) bully, won't spot me but my efforts are in vain as he and his three sidekicks are already on their way over.

'Show us some of the karate you've been learning,' one says.

'Nah, karate is for sissies,' another yells.

'Come on, Albert, show him. His moves mean nothing,' the first one mocks.

Albert walks towards me and asks, 'Are you going to fight back this time?'

Before I can answer, he hits me on the nose with his head. I can taste the blood as it runs down to my mouth. I'm petrified. He is bigger, stronger and dumber ... and he is standing right in front of me waiting for me to react.

Today I'm going to have to back myself. No-one is going to stop him and no-one is going to help me ...

I'm not going to go for a lucky punch because that will just upset him and he will be back terrorising me the following day. I'm going to have to do this the right way. I'm going to have to back myself. I step back, raise my fists and say, 'You asked for this.'

He launches forward towards me with a punch. I pull my front foot towards my back foot, turn and extend my leg, executing the perfect back kick to his solar plexus, which I follow up with a roundhouse kick to the side of his head. I've dropped him and a few seconds later I am standing over him saying, 'If you want we can do this again tomorrow.' I have transcended from victim to victor – I backed myself.

Ironically, most of the occasions on which you will have to back yourself won't take the form of a physical and somewhat barbaric gladiator-like battle. The toughest battles will be in your mind, and will involve your willpower, your perseverance and your determination to overcome those odds that stand in the way of your ability to learn and grow on this path that you have chosen for yourself.

In the spirit of bringing balance to this introduction, one afternoon during my first year at university, I saw a blind fellow student who looked lost. I walked over and asked him if I could help. He asked me to just point him in the direction of the hostels. I offered to walk with him, but he declined. He said he needed to find his own way as he had already practised the route. I then offered just to walk behind him in case he got lost. Again he thanked me but said that with me as a back-up, he would cut himself too much slack. He said, 'I have to back myself on this otherwise I'm going to struggle for too long to find my way around campus.'

I walked away thinking that this is what you call not taking the easy way out and backing yourself so that your future may be easier.

As you are reading this, I'll bet there are a few stories flashing past your screen of consciousness of either yourself or someone you know who backed themselves to get through some kind of adversity, and by doing that not only overcame adversity, but became a better person as a result of the experience.

This book is not just about overcoming adversity and getting through tough times. It's about how to create a better future, how to build patterns that will serve you in the future. The story about the school bully is not about a fight or a lucky shot. It's about years of training four times a week at a dojo, hours of sparring with different opponents. It's about paging through and reading hundreds of karate magazines and even watching the beloved Bruce Lee movies over and over again.

The blind student's story is about walking on the campus, counting steps, finding orientation, hearing voices at the cafeteria, climbing stairs at the auditorium ... over and over and over again until it all becomes familiar territory.

Week after week I receive mails, calls and people asking if there is some kind of formula one can apply to get what you want, to do what you love, to get paid for it and to make a difference. The short answer is 'YES'. I know you could have guessed that answer. What you really want to know is HOW? This book is all about HOW.

In sharing the HOW with you, I am going to use a lot of 'poetic licence'.

I am going to give you numbers and concepts you can add or subtract from. In other words, they are not cast in stone. They come from my experience and the experience of some great men and women whom I hold in high regard.

While I'm writing this I'm watching a documentary on Floyd Mayweather, the undefeated boxer. The interviewer has asked him how many sit-ups he does per day and he has said 2 000. Well, we don't know if he does 1 900 or 2 500 a day but we do know he does a hell of a lot of them. In boxing as in life, there is no exact number, so bear in mind that a number is an indication and not a formula.

Here is your chance to banish all your excuses, to show up for yourself and to back yourself to become who you came here to be. By the end of this book you will be able to say a lot of things, but one thing you will not be able to say is, 'I didn't know how to do it' because once you know how you can never again not know.

If you would rather live with excuses for the rest of your life, now is the time to stop reading. If you choose to do so on the basis that you don't like the writing or the author or you don't need help or whatever other excuse you would like to use, it's fine with me. But if you continue, know that you will be called out to back yourself and prove that you are what you can be.

Go ahead and choose NOW.

If you know too little about your subject matter, sooner or later you will be caught out by the smart group.

GET GOING

There are many words and concepts for this simple act of getting going, possibly because so many people find it extremely difficult to take this step.

In my case, during my university days, I would do everything I could to delay starting to study. I would clean my room, organise my notes, make photocopies, make my bed, stack the reference books on my desk, refer to the tips for effective study given by the lecturer and perform many, many other actions (excuses) before I would put my bum down on the chair and start studying.

This chapter could actually fit in anywhere in this book because there is nothing as powerful as getting going. So whatever it takes to start, kick off, get going, begin, strip, play, sell, open, try, shoot ahead or whatever you choose to call it, do it – NOW.

Many books have been written about the power of momentum and movement. You don't have to read any of them if you can succeed in finding a way to get past all those seemingly smart but truly pathetic excuses and just get going.

They say life rewards action. Getting going is all about making the move and taking action. Thinking about something and talking about it is great, but the real value lies in the 'doing'.

WHAT TURNS YOU ON?

What is it that does it for you?

All of us are in some way turned on by something. It could be something we look forward to such as a holiday or a trip to an exotic destination.

When we window shop we dream about buying beautiful things for ourselves and our homes. We are turned on by beauty, success, achievement, pride, being healthy and so forth, but that's not what I am asking you.

My question to you is much deeper and more profound than the suggestions mentioned above.

Ask yourself this: Why do you want to get up in the morning, besides answering the call of Mother Nature to empty your bladder? What is calling you either by whispering your name or shouting it? This is a hard question and most people I know cannot give a straight answer to it. They can mumble around how they want to feel when they find it ... happy, excited, energised, etc, but they cannot say 'this' is what turns me on. Many people sit in corporate offices making someone else's dream come true, not realising they have the power to live that calling or vocation right there in corporate life or not realising they have overstayed their welcome. They are now stealing someone else's money because they don't know what turns them on and that they need to learn how to back themselves to live the life they want.

Explore, push, ask, push harder

This book will be of so much more value to you if you can put your finger on what it is that really excites you, what it is that stirs your nervous system and ignites the fire in your belly.

Identifying exactly what that may be is difficult, but there are ways to force the mind and the heart to work for you until you get an answer.

Note that we are talking about 'an answer' because that answer may change. You may be counting your money from selling shoes and find that you would prefer to be an accountant, or an investor, or a dealmaker.

The tips are simple:

1.   Explore – the more you expose yourself to different interests and possibilities, the more information you will have at your disposal to make a decision based on what excites your interest and feels right for you.
2.   Ask – have conversations about all sorts of things. You will feel your pulse racing if you start to talk about something that you have a feeling and a flair for. Then ask more questions about it and go back to the first point – explore.
3.   Push and push harder:
   - Do volunteer work.
   - Attend seminars.
   - Read.
   - Remain open.
   - Feel what resonates with you.
   - Think.

Remember, this is your life we are talking about. You want to get this right. You don't want to settle for some mediocre job where your only compensation is that you get paid enough to cover the bills and go on leave once a year, with a medical aid and 50/50 pension. No, the world is changing. Those jobs are fast disappearing and becoming obsolete in the new economy.

I urge you to push harder to find what it is that makes you feel fully alive and pursue it. As you read on, this book will help you to find out how to make a success of 'it', but first you are going to have to find what 'it' is.

DON'T READ A BOOK, READ MORE THAN 200 BOOKS

Knowledge is NOT power ...

No, it isn't power – keeping what you know in your head and processing it up there day after day is really not that powerful. In fact it could actually drain your power (energy).

Knowledge is potential power and it's only when you can see how to apply what you have learned in life and then apply it effectively, that knowledge becomes truly powerful.

Reading 200 (plus) books

Many years ago I met a genius – his name is Rudi Kruger. A few things impressed me about Rudi. First of all, he had a library of books and magazines that stunned me. I have never seen such a large private collection of publications in my life. The second thing that impressed me was that he had read them all and that he could integrate the relevant points of a number of books and come up with a brilliant answer or interpretation on a specific subject using not only his own insight, but also the accumulated knowledge contained in these books.

I had the opportunity to spend quite a lot of time with Rudi and he often told me that before I can claim to know anything about any subject, I need to read at least 200 books on that subject. I never asked him why specifically

200 books. I guess this has something to do with the 10 000- hour principle Malcolm Gladwell talks about in his book *The Outliers.*

According to this principle, any successful person needs to spend at least 10 000 hours learning his or her craft.

My third year at university

During my third year at university, a friend of my dad's, Dan Seymour, came to visit me. I took him on a tour of the campus and while I was showing him the library he asked which books we were studying in our third-year psychology course. I showed him the three or four prescribed books and he wanted to know whether we studied every chapter in the book. Of course not, I explained. He then wanted to know if I had at least read all the chapters in the books. Again I explained that this wasn't required reading. He then asked whether I had read some of the other hundred or so books on psychology on the library's bookshelves. 'No' was my answer again.

He then looked me straight in the eye and said, 'Your dad pays good money for you to attend this university and you think you can study as little as possible instead of studying as much as possible so that you can be smarter than the rest of your peers. I am disappointed in you, Rinus.'

That conversation changed my view of studying forever. The smart people learn as much as possible. The average people do an average amount of studying. The really not-so-smart people try to get away with studying as little as possible.

It's more than books

In Rudi's library there were thousands and thousands of magazines,

DVDs and published articles on subjects as diverse as business, psychology, architecture, design, health and others. There are many other sources of information that contribute to one's insight and knowledge about this interconnected world we live in.

Connect the dots

You will see that I often refer to this point of connecting dots. Connecting dots is what I call a higher-order cognitive skill. It is the ability to connect relevant information gathered from a number of sources and to form one's own opinion on the basis of that information.

With time and practice, the skills involved in connecting the dots can be developed. When you start seeing certain patterns or trends in, for instance, business or in nature, you are developing the scarce skill of integration. By being able to spot these patterns or trends, your chances of survival and success in the future become so much better. You could become someone others would want to consult about a number of aspects of their personal and business lives because of your superior ability to integrate information and thereby to be able to offer a more educated opinion.

At this point you begin to see that all things – both physical and nonphysical – are linked and that there are connections between design, business, the economy, politics, consumer behaviour, spiritualism, love, hate and everything else that exists. Those who can make these connections are better equipped to focus attention on them and in this way to contribute towards the solution of complex problems.

Most importantly, the ability to forge these links puts you in touch with your true potential. You begin to think and act on a higher plane and at this point you know that your investment in studying, reading, etc has begun to pay off.

Everyone likes 'confident', but no-one likes 'arrogant'.

WATCH MORE THAN 50 HOURS OF FOOTAGE ON HOW IT'S DONE

Audiovisual media

We are lucky that we are living in the audiovisual age. Thanks to modern-day technology, everything from wars, stand-up comedy and mishaps to great political and social announcements is downloadable and almost instantaneously available in audiovisual form. The human mind responds well to audiovisual learning, especially when the viewer has an interest in a specific topic.

Stuff to watch and where to find it

If you know your way around the internet, you will find an almost inexhaustible array of audiovisual material pertaining to all your interests.

If you are looking for insight from some of the great masters of cuisine, spirituality, business and more, I would suggest you look at:

1. YouTube
2. TED Talks
3. Talk shows hosted by such well-known people as Piers Morgan, Jay Leno, Oprah, Charlie Rose, etc

What to look for

When I watch footage I look out for:

1. the style of presentation
2. how presenters express themselves
3. body language
4. quality of content
5. other aspects of communication such as tone of voice, facial expression and duration of talk.

You can learn a lot about engaging an audience just by observing how comedians such as Chris Rock and Billy Connelly work the crowd.

Great speakers such as Tony Robbins and Zig Ziglar use equally powerful techniques to get a point across, and by watching footage of all these greats, you will learn how to project your energy and show your passion.

It is also true that by watching less effective communicators you can learn just as much regarding what to avoid.

The more footage you watch, the easier it will become to use the knowledge or information you glean to become a sharper presenter.

Know a lot but never think you know it all – you
never will.

HAVE MORE THAN 100 CONVERSATIONS WITH PEOPLE SMARTER THAN YOU

Everyone is smarter than you

When it comes to an attitude of learning, it's good to have the mindset that you can learn from every single person on the planet. What is more, you can learn from animals and nature too, if you pay attention.

For example, I believe that our female cat, Bongi, is smarter than the average cat and what amazes me most is her patience. If she wants to jump onto the bed, she will either wait until the dogs have settled down so that they don't bother her, or until I have found my most comfortable position in bed. She will then softly make her way over to me and fall asleep in a place where she knows she won't be disturbed. Certainly smarter than me ... I have little patience and want things to happen fast, often to my own detriment.

Have the questions ready

With every conversation you have where the intention is for you to learn and grow, make sure you have the relevant questions ready. I often ponder on what questions I would ask such famous personalities as Desmond Tutu, Stephen Hawking, Richard Branson, Jimmy Page, Seth Godin, Deepak Chopra, etc if I ever had the opportunity. One thing I know for sure is that I wouldn't make the same mistake as the well-known talk show host in South

Africa who interviewed Bob Geldof and asked him if he likes music ... opportunity missed.

I recently completed a contract at an engineering firm where part of the agreement was that I would interview five selected members of the management team. Unexpectedly, however, the HR Manager who attended the group session appeared. She explained that although she was not on the list she actually wanted to ask me a few questions. Irene was prepared. She opened her book and I could see her list of eight or ten handwritten questions. She was excited to learn and gather information and the two hours spent with Irene passed much more pleasantly than the five hours I spent with the selected managers. She had decided on what she wanted to know and made sure she got the answers.

Go for the story

In his book *A Whole New Mind* Daniel H Pink explains us that we are now more driven by the stories of our lives than anything else. In most of my other books I've included lessons learned and stories told by ordinary people who have inspired me. I want to give you the same advice I received years ago and that is 'Go for the story'. Whoever you speak to can give you 10% of the value he or she has to offer by giving you facts, but if he/she decides to share their story, you are getting the real deal. If you learn to listen between the lines, you will not only get the facts, but also the emotion, the intent, the soul of what it is you are after.

Find a few mentors

One is not enough. You want to have constructive conversations with mentors about your career, your finances, your personal development, your personal life, and possibly about a few other things too.

I cannot begin to thank the mentors I have in my life. Some I had to beg to mentor me, some offered, but all of them have added massive value.

The important thing is to become a worthy mentee. Don't waste their time. Try following their suggestions and give them honest feedback.

As the Buddhist saying goes: 'When the student is ready, the teacher will appear.'

Network

Whenever I think or write about networking, I wish I could introduce you to my friend Timothy Webster. Tim is a master when it comes to networking. He connects with people by meeting with them and he also connects people with each other by setting up meetings for those with similar interests and mandates. This takes effort and energy and you may not always be in the mood for it but go – go network – it will pay off in the long run.

One tip about networking: if the people with whom you attempt to network pick up even the vaguest hint that all you want are their contacts and experience, you are dead in the water. If you are out there just to take, you are in big trouble. You have to have something to give.

Having read this book up to this point, by now you will know that you have a lot to give – insight, a few tips, an uplifting story about someone else, and much more.

If fear is your partner rather than love, she will let you down time and time again.

WHAT NO-ONE BOTHERED TO TEACH YOU

What went wrong?

The answer is a paradoxical one. Everything went wrong and nothing went wrong. You just need to go onto YouTube or TED Talks and type in 'education' to get the whole story.

The education system is geared towards providing the industrial system with people who can 'fit in' with it. These are people who can punch a clock card, do a job and punch out again, and can be replaced at any time without delaying or disturbing the production process. You are a small cog in a great machine. You are trained to perform that function and you get paid for that.

To keep the industrial machine going, you need supervisors and managers to oversee the process and ensure that all runs smoothly and according to plan. These technical, supervisory and managerial people need training.

So we adapt the education system accordingly: students are processed from one grade to another and are given a pass mark by 'the company' if they get it right. We teach them discipline, to walk in queues and not to ask too many questions. A student who steps out of line is in trouble.

He or she will then be held back and re-processed, or be labelled as a troublemaker and be processed more harshly, or in extreme cases, be put onto medication to ensure compliance.

One way or another, compliance with the system is thus enforced not only at schools but also at technical colleges and universities.

These graduates then apply for jobs in the 'system'. They are given a machine to work, an office to sit in, an annual vacation to rest, a salary each month, medical aid and the promise of a pension at the end of their 30 or 40 years of loyal hard work. Do you get the picture?

What about the teachers?

Teachers are trained or 'processed' to produce students who can meet the needs of the individual economy. They are part of the system. They, in turn, 'process' their students through each stage of the system. It's the way the system was designed.

If you've watched the movie *Dead Poets Society* with Robin Williams, you will have seen how this works and how the best teachers are sidelined to make space for those who comply with the system. What is worse is that teachers generally don't earn high salaries, so they're unlikely to rebel against the system and make trouble. No, they are like factory staff. They are paid just enough to get by and to keep the dream of a pension and a fairly comfortable old age alive.

Connecting the dots

All great statesmen and leaders win votes and touch the hearts of nations by reiterating how important education is. At the same time, all parents want a better life for their children. Therefore they trust that their political leaders will invest a sufficient portion of taxpayers' money in the school system to ensure that their children receive a quality education – a school system that should be revised to say the least.

We are living in the technological age, in the information age, and we have still not revised the schooling system to keep pace with that. Socalled 'Generation Y' individuals are now young adults and are entering an unpredictable 'knowledge economy' where access to technology is taken for granted and where creativity and innovative thinking are valued above mere competence in subjects studied at secondary or tertiary level. Yet we are still not teaching students to connect the dots.

An A for English and maybe a D for Maths and C or E for Science. Well, at least the student can speak and write in English, but we need to teach students how to connect the A, B, C, D and E. Their symbols for subjects don't stand in isolation to one another. If a student gets an A for Maths and a D for English, everyone is convinced she should enrol for a degree related to the sciences. But has anyone explained to her the relevance of language when it comes to expressing her talent and skills? Does the young man who got an A for English and E for Maths know that Shakespeare was a genius in the field of mathematics, that Pythagoras was a great philosopher and that Pascal wrote the most beautiful essays?

This fragmented approach to learning will not help us to succeed in the future. The key is context. The key is to learn how to connect the dots.

In Sir Ken Robinson's book *Out of Our Minds*, he explains how important it is to rethink education to particularly stimulate creativity and explore new ways of using our minds to create a different and better future.

What's the solution?

Start un-learning!!! Create a new mindset with new learning objectives where you can ask questions and not be afraid to be wrong, where you 'must' make mistakes so that you can learn as a result of them. Stimulate creativity in the mind to identify new challenges and to come up with new solutions. Commit to life-long learning and take the decision to actively learn until the day you die. Challenge everything and find the answers that work for you. Never ever be afraid to try something new.

Sir Ken Robinson tells the story of a little girl who was instructed by her teacher to draw something. The teacher asked her what she was going to draw and she said she was going to draw a picture of God. Fairly worried, the teacher explained that no-one on earth really knows what God looks like. The girl confidently replied: 'They will in a few minutes.

Steer clear of belittling yourself or others.

35

LEARN TO COUNT

Numbers count

As much as this book is about knowledge and getting ahead in life, no matter what the circumstances, numbers do count. If you have put in all the work to live your passion and to make a difference, it might be worth your while to learn about and understand finances.

Putting together any deal has to do with energy – the energy you put into your products and services and the money/energy you receive in return for them. Learning how to structure a deal, perceiving the advantages for yourself and for your clients, making sure the value proposition is mutually beneficial, are all elements better understood when you have mastered an understanding of finances.

Can you hear the notes?

When you look at a sheet of music you may, like me, see absolutely nothing but lines and funny characters they call notes. I cannot make sense of it nor hear the music it represents. Yet the musician and the conductor are able to 'hear' the symphony by reading the notes. It is the same with a balance sheet or a tax-return form or a financial project.

Some of us can grasp the advantages of a deal, understand the related finances, gauge how healthy or unhealthy a business is, how good a project looks and whether cost and profits are realistic and reachable.

This ability to 'hear the notes' will serve you and compliment your skills as a business person.

To my mind one of the most inspiring writers in the world is Richard Bach who has written many books including *Jonathan Livingston Seagull* and *Illusions*. Right at the beginning of his successful career, he lost a fortune due to non-interest in his finances. The fact is that if you really have nointerest in 'hearing the notes' on the balance sheet, you should hire someone who can do it for you. You would be a fool not to attempt to understand or alternatively have your finances explained to you. If you don't you may just lose everything you have worked for, and that is most definitely not what backing yourself is about.

All addictions will harm you - whether they
are to alcohol, sex, power, attention, drugs
or money.

DON'T STRESS ABOUT THE BLIND SNIPER

A blind sniper ...?

Yes. These 'snipers' are trigger happy. All they want to do is shoot something down. Whether it's a good, average or bad idea, they will take a shot at it. To be blunt, these are the fools of the world who will never show us their art. They will never have any skin in the game, but they will claim to know exactly why what you do and how you are doing it will never work.

I call them 'blind snipers' because they have a weapon and ammunition but they also have a blindfold on. They hear something and pull the trigger. They will turn up in your life when you get going. A 'blind sniper' could be a family member, a friend or a colleague. Their main objective is to shoot everything down. Don't pay any attention to them. They are a bunch of fearful fools.

The best you can do is not to argue with them or try to sway their opinion. Stay as far away from them as you possibly can. You don't need them in your life.

CREATE A HOT WEBSITE

Got to have one

Some people create websites for their babies on the day of their birth and post all the photos and good wishes received there year by year. As far as I know, nobody has spoken to any of these children to ask how they feel about it but that is beside the point. The point is that everyone should have a web page. Whether you are working for a corporate or for yourself, it's a good idea to have a site or a page where, over and above your social media stuff, you get to own your identity.

The question is … can we find you? Whether you are an electrician, plumber, violinist, psychologist or breeder of exotic cats, we should be able to find you. So it seems obvious that if you are going to back yourself, you will need some sort of landing pad for your identity.

Investigate options

It would be wise to read up about the best format and in which 'language' to develop a site. Some of this development can be done by you, but as your site becomes more integrative, you may have to use a web developer to do a good job for you.

Plan on what you want the site to achieve and take your time to spec it carefully so that you have the functionality you need and can add on as required. This is important if you are to avoid sticking with one developer for life. It's better to keep your options open without being totally committed to one genius who has all the codes for your site.

Create value

A good site has something new on offer. You want people to come back, even if the only reasons they visit your site are to see the weather prediction for the city and to read a quirky comment from your side.

People are looking for value and if you can get them to view your site for any reason, you can grab their attention and give them value, get them to visit it again and possibly enlist them among your followers. Especially if the value you offer is for free, they will return to your site time and again. Remember the saying, 'In the world of the drug lord the first shot is always for free.'

Once you figure out how to create value and to get people to come back to your site because of that value, you've got it made.

You will win respect by showing respect.

44

START WRITING

So you can't write

You may not be the next JK Rowling or have the literary abilities of a Wilbur Smith or William Shakespeare, but write anyway – you *can* write.

When I was in Grade 11 my English teacher told my parents that I would never have any command over either the spoken or written word in the

English language. This curse was only broken when I met my first English speaking girlfriend whose parents couldn't speak a word of Afrikaans.

I quickly learned to handle myself and they had no mercy. If I made a mistake, they always corrected me.

Even today my writing will never be considered for any literary prize, but I have a great editor who corrects any structural mistakes and makes my work acceptable. Thus, the excuse that you cannot write simply no longer holds water. You can find online editors who, for a small fee, will help you to express your ideas clearly.

Why writing?

It is a way to get your ideas out there – remember, your opinion counts.

This is all about backing yourself, so in order to communicate your opinion to others, you must be willing to open up and be vulnerable.

One cannot write about writing and not mention Seth Godin. He publishes a blog post daily for free. He has written a number of books and his followers look forward to every blog post and every book. He is reputed to have one of the greatest number of followers in the world.

Fact is he must have started somewhere. He too has had a first blog post, a first article, a first book. Write, write, write – you will not be sorry.

Where should you publish your work?

This answer is as you would expect – anywhere you can. If you are writing for a corporate, do your best to get your contribution into the monthly or weekly corporate publications. Start writing on the intranet.

Get staff members to subscribe to your work.

Otherwise:

1.   Start writing a blog or blogs.
2.   Write for the electronic media.
3.   Submit your writing to your local newspaper.
4.   Write comments.
5.   Use social media platforms for your output.

You can also, if you so choose, write a book. There are a few options regarding publication here:

1.   Look for a publisher.
2.   Create an e-book.
3.   Self-publish.

Download the book APE: Author, Publisher, Entrepreneur by Guy Kawasaki and get his advice on how to get a book published. This is really worthwhile reading and will give you valuable insight into how to go about it.

It has become increasingly easy to get your stuff out there. The question is: Do you have something worthwhile to say and do you know people who would want to hear more from you because you are adding value to their lives? That is the big question. You won't know the answer until you try. Go ahead and give it a shot.

What should you write about?

Nobody has the authority or should have the audacity to tell you what you should write about but, and it is a small but, consider the following when it comes to subject matter:

1. that area in which you are a thought leader
2. those fields in which you feel your opinion can add value
3. those issues that you feel strongly about
4. those things you have observed but don't think others have spotted
5. anything you think may give someone insight, provoke a reaction or put a smile on someone's face.

There you have a few points to ponder.

CREATE A FOLLOWING

Why a following?

In the new economy where connection is everything, this will be the only way you will survive in business and please note that this is not only if you have your own small or major business. These principles apply as much to individuals in organisations. If you have people respecting you, seeking your advice and admiring you for how you do your work, you have a following. That means you are doing something that people can identify with on a deeper level – they 'feel' you. Once people 'feel' you, they become loyal and they will do whatever they can to promote and support you.

It's easier than ever

The Beatles sold over 2 billion albums in their heyday. This was before I-tunes, downloads and all other forms of obtaining digital files. When John Lennon said, 'We are more popular than Jesus', I don't know if he checked his facts, but there's no doubt that the Beatles had a massive following all over the world.

Celebrities have millions of people following them on Twitter, Facebook and other social media platforms. Artists release a song and moments later there are millions of downloads.

Your cat falls into the fishbowl and tens of thousands of people see it on YouTube – your cat has a following.

In the old economy, marketing campaigns had to be started up and supported by massive PR campaigns to create a following. In the connection economy, the keyword is 'following' so everyone with a smartphone can create a following.

Create your tribe

If you read Seth Godin's book called *Tribes* or Joseph Campbell's books on mythology, you will see that in some way we all 'want' to belong to a tribe. Yes, we may have tendered our resignation from our more traditional tribes, but if you subscribe to the blog of Guy Kawasaki, for example, you are a member of his tribe.

The people who read what you write, listen to what you say and seek what you seek are part of your tribe. They subscribe to your opinion and your thinking, and you have a responsibility towards them. That is to be true to yourself and true to what you believe. Should your beliefs and understandings change, it is your duty to tell your followers so that it becomes their prerogative as to whether they want to remain in the tribe or leave. They might just choose to celebrate your new insights with you and subsequently strengthen the cohesion of the tribe.

I belong to a number of tribes and get something special from each of them. If you do something that grabs my attention, I will be more than willing to become a member of your tribe too, provided you create that connection that I and all other potential followers are looking for.

The social media myth

It is important to know that the followers on social media sites are not all real followers. Even though celebrities like Beyonce and Led Zeppelin probably have a few million followers on social media, should they release a new album, this doesn't necessarily mean that the majority of their followers will go out and buy it. They may 'like' a track and write something about it, which in itself is not a bad thing, but it doesn't translate into sales or revenue of some kind.

Don't live under the illusion that a social media follower is necessarily a loyal member of your tribe who will act as an evangelist for you.

How shall I create a following then?

1. Be true to yourself.
2. Practise your art.
3. Add value.
4. Make a difference.
5. Offer something unique or in a unique way.
6. Respect your followers.

THE FEAR OF DEATH

What is the fear of death really?

It is fear of the unknown. We fear it because there is no certainty about what lies beyond it. I don't want us to ponder the nature of life or death in this chapter, but rather to use the fear of death as a metaphor for fear of change. Most companies and individuals fear change because for them it is the end of a certain way of doing things and there is no certainty regarding what is beyond what they know and what they have become accustomed to.

Time to 'die'

For you to get to the point where you are willing to back yourself, to take a chance and to try what has been suggested up to now in this book, you will have to 'die'. Yes, 'die' in the sense of abandoning the life you have lived up until now. Are you afraid? Of course you are. So was everyone who came before you and everyone who will come after you.

Human beings tend to mistrust uncertainty and are reluctant to leave behind that which they know and know how to do. Why do you think so few artists follow their bliss, so few students study what really interests them, so few new authors start writing, so few people stand up and speak their mind, so few philanthropists give their millions to the poor and broken? The answer is that they are afraid. They know they will have to allow the old self to 'die' and that they will have to be reborn to a new self they know nothing about. There will be no certainty.

There will be no guarantees and there will be no safety net, but in their stead there will be a feeling of aliveness, of making a difference, of true authenticity, of being real, of being vulnerable and of being bold in the face of fear and death.

Are you afraid? You should be, but do it anyway. Back yourself.

Both not being sensitive enough and being over-sensitive are weaknesses of the ego.

TRAVEL

Why travel?

Whether you are eighteen or eighty-five, travel is always an important eye opener and an excellent educator. Why? Because it makes you aware in ways no-one can explain to you. When you observe and interact with people who have different values and cultures from your own, it broadens your mind. You begin to understand that the world is much bigger and more complex than you could have imagined and your awareness expands in different directions.

It may be expensive but travel is a wonderful way to grow your understanding of yourself and of the world you live in. One thing is for sure: travel affords you the opportunity to see your life and life in general in context. We all need more context. We all need to have experiences that are different from the ones we are used to because this educates us and gives us deeper understanding. That's what we need to learn and grow ourselves.

Where to?

Before you decide that you must experience European, Asian or American culture, start off by travelling to the places around you, or even on your own continent. As a first step, consider paying a visit to the adjoining neighbourhood in the area in which you live if you've never visited it before. Yes, if are living in South Africa where I live, and you are surrounded by many other cultures, dedicate yourself to visiting the places where their tribes gather. Observe how your fellow countrymen live and what is important to them. For example, it often shocks me that many people in my country have never seen the sea.

By all means go and visit other continents too; all travel will enhance your life. Yes, you have the internet and good travel programmes on television and you are connected to friends all over the world, but go, go travel, expand your horizons. It will serve you well.

What will you learn?

A lot more than can be told in a short book like this, but here are a few magical lessons to learn:

1. How big and yet how small the world is.
2. How we are all so different yet so much alike.
3. That there is much more to life than you thought there was.
4. What you take for granted, others envy and what you envy, others take for granted.
5. Most of all, your eyes will open inwards and you will see more of yourself.

Go ahead and spread your wings.

If you are going to lie, know that there will always be consequences to face.

THE TURNAROUND

The prophet of doom

Every business and every sort of tribe has a prophet of doom. This is the person who stands on the top of the mountain and declares to the tribe that the end is near – whether it is the enemy who is approaching, the tsunami that will destroy the village, the new technology that will never work or even the new manager who was appointed to begin the retrenchment process. You will find them in all walks of life. They are self-appointed and their *raison d'être* is to tell you the bad news or how things will never be better.

I started a new project at a government agency which involved working with a member of top management on how to influence and inspire their staff. As I walked into his office, he told me that throughout his career he has seen many of my kind and they have all failed. He became my personal challenge and my contract was for 18 months, so you can imagine how much of my personal attention he received. (Also see the chapter entitled 'The Blind Sniper'.)

There is always a way back

There is a way back from negativity to positivity. We are not rigid machines. We are human beings and if there is enough personal motivation and desire to change our ways, we do so. The good news is that if you are the prophet of doom, know that there is a way to turn it all around and change your behaviour.

The primary reason why people stick to their current attitudes or behaviour is that they are not aware that there is a way out. They therefore sink deeper and deeper into these self-perpetuating patterns of thinking and acting. Yet if alcoholics, drug addicts, criminals and others who display destructive behaviour can find a way back to normality and a more positive life, it is definitely possible for the prophet of doom to do the same.

Why the turnaround?

It is because you owe it to yourself. Sinking deeper and deeper into your own negative dung is not a life and if you choose that, you are missing out on a wonderful life. We all have our off-days, and we all look at life from time to time with a speck of doubt and scepticism, and there is nothing wrong with that. But if you make negativity your way of life because of your ego issues, you should reconsider your attitude towards yourself and your life.

There is truly a much better life available to you if you choose to start backing yourself and changing your behaviour.

How to do it

If you are serious about doing a turnaround, here are some very practicalsuggestions to follow:

1. Start with an internal process. Read about people who live positive lives and become aware of the positive things in your own life.
2. Commit to live a life of gratitude. Take time daily to be thankful for what you have and who you are.
3. Whenever you see evidence of the 'negative' and want to react, hold back. Don't express your negative observation.
4. Now you can start making positive comments on the positive things you observe. At first you don't even have to do so out loud. Just do it in your mind. Later on you can start verbalising it.

5. Here is the most difficult part. When you observe negative things at work or at home, ask yourself, 'How can I turn this around? What is there to learn? How can I grow from this observation?'
6. It's often wise to admit it when you can't see the positive, but then at least commit to gathering more information and getting some context.
7. Know that we all experience negative things. The key to the turnaround is in how to react to them and how not to allow them to contaminate our lives.

You may well not morph overnight from the prophet of doom to the angel of hope, but with dedication from your side, anything is possible.

Go ahead and do the turnaround.

LOOK THE PART

What to wear

Both in the corporate and non-corporate world, how you dress has an effect on the people around you. The topic is much more complex than 'what to wear and what not to wear'. There are elements of:

1. dress requirements or dress code
2. personal style
3. group conformity
4. personal perceptions and perceived perceptions of others.

All of these factors play a role in how we dress.

While reading through a few quotes on dress sense and the do's and don'ts of dressing for specific contexts and occasions, I came across this quote By Bianca Frazier that impressed me enough to put it in this book: 'Dress how you want to be addressed.'

Think about the judges and advocates in court and businessmen with different styles of dress such as Donald Trump vs Richard Branson, the investment banker vs the retailer. Perhaps there is more to the quote than meets the eye. Perhaps we dress up because we want to be 'addressed' in that way, but it may also be because we think that is how others would expect us to dress if we want to be addressed in a certain way ... Food for thought.

Dress the part but pull it off

There are few things more embarrassing than to see someone in an outfit they bought for a special event, but they simply fail to pull it off. You can see how mentally uncomfortable they are with the attire. We often think that in order to fit in or to stand out, we need a certain 'suit'. That's fine, get the 'suit' or the dress but make sure you can pull it off. It's fine if you can make it 'you' and wear it with authenticity. If not, reconsider the outfit.

Dress your mind and manners as well as you dress the rest of you

We have all witnessed the guy or girl dressed for success who goes overboard at a party and spoils it all with bad manners.

We have also seen the person who receives the invitation for the way they dress but parks their brain with their flashy car in the basement parking.

The message is simple. Work on the package deal. It is said that 'clothes make the man', but only if you have the manners to match. The one without the other will make you look like a fool.

Thank you, Madiba

We have the late Mr Nelson Mandela to thank for a lot of things and one of them is for introducing the 'Madiba shirt'. At last we are free to dress more 'African' than 'European' and in warm weather that is such a blessing.

Maintain a strong work ethic.

PRACTISE COMMON DECENCY

What is it?

Common decency is basically doing what is expected of a normal human being. That's what Yahoo says it is and it seems to be a fair definition.

We all live by different sets of values and principles, and that is great, but there are a number of core principles and behaviours we find in all religions, cultures and sub-cultures. This is the 'common' behaviour that most of us subscribe to if we are normal human beings. When we follow these common principles of behaviour, we all live together more peacefully and harmoniously, and it serves us all better to do so.

In the little book called *All I really need to know I learned at kindergarten* Robert Fulghum explains that most of the social behaviours and principles that make for a cohesive society are taught at kindergarten, but get lost as we grow up and begin to fight for our place in adult society.

You will agree that observing these very basic rules of common decency will make the world a better place:

1. When entering or leaving a space where there are other people, always say 'hello' and 'goodbye'.
2. Practise what mom taught you by using the words 'please' and 'thank you'.
3. When making eye contact, be the first to smile.
4. Don't take what isn't yours.
5. Share with others.

6. Be kind to older people.
7. Kneel down when you interact with small children.
8. Be thankful for what you have and show it.
9. Tell the people you love that you love them – often.
10. If it's good, acknowledge it.
11. Do unto others what you would want them to do unto you.

Consider these behaviours going forward in life. They come with a common guarantee. If you practise them your life will be better than if you don't.

All your good work can be equally destroyed by impatience on the one hand and procrastination on the other.

FAIL FORWARD

To fail or not to fail

Most cultures, businesses and schools will tell you that the less often you fail, the more successful you are. Yet being wired to succeed and wanting to make a success of your life do not mean you should frown upon failure.

If you are going to give the opportunity to succeed only one shot and not try again or be completely defeated by failure, you will be led to the false belief that if you fail, you are screwed for life. But if you, like all other human beings, have the ability to try again, get over your failures, persevere and learn from your mistakes, failure may actually not be such a bad thing for you. It is generally known and accepted that we learn more about our trade or art and ourselves when we fail than when we succeed.

How to fail

I guess the title of this chapter says it all. If you are going to fail, do it forward. At least in that way you are on winning ground. The guru John C

Maxwell's book, *Failing Forward*, will tell you to use failures as stepping stones, to learn from failure and to move on. One can, with a great degree of certainty, say that most people do not go out of their way to fail, but that's not the point of how to fail. The point is one's attitude and mindset towards failure. If we know that some degree of failure is inevitable and if we know, in some wonderful way, that with the right mindset we will be able to benefit from failure, it becomes easier to digest. How to fail?

Forward, and learn from it ... that is the long and the short of failing.

Direction, focus and failure

It's always easier to work through failure if you know you are going in the right direction and are focusing on an objective you are working towards.

Failure tends to harm us much more if we are uncertain of what it is we want in life and we are not really focused. To use a simple analogy, it's more difficult to stand up if you don't know why you are standing up and if you are up, in which direction you are going.

Knowing that creates something of a safety net, or possibly a break-fall technique so that you don't just crash and burn. Here are a few pointers:

1. Take time to determine what it is you really, really, really want in life.
2. Have a clear sense of direction.
3. Keep your focus. If you are going to lose focus every time you fail, you are not going to get far in life. So – focus, focus, focus.

Giving up is not an option

Most of us have been there, whether it was in our own business, or at work, or perhaps in our personal lives. At one time or another, so many of us have experienced that hopeless feeling and said to ourselves, 'I cannot go on – I am defeated.' During these times individuals tend to turn to religion, friends and family, often to drugs and alcohol, and most often it is a combination of a few of these proverbial crutches that we grab at.

Personally, I have been there. I've seen the darkness without any glimmer of light. The one thing I've always pondered over is this: If I give up now, what is it that I will do in the next minute? What do you do after you have given up? Go and lie under the duvet, cry, tear your clothes, and curse the world and everyone and everything in it? What does one do?

Of course, taking your own life is an option, but heed the words of a professor I once saw on the Charlie Rose show on Bloomberg TV who said,

'Suicide is a permanent solution to a temporary problem.'

From my personal point of view, I'm just not sure the darkness and emptiness and failure will end with taking one's life – just my opinion.

So giving up is not really an option, as moments later the doorbell may ring, or your nose will be itchy and you will have to give up giving up.

So here is a suggestion. If you feel you have to give up, go ahead and do so for a while. Take a break. Curse if you have to. Cry if it will make you feel better. Do what you have to, but remain aware that deep inside all of us there is something so for real and so strong that it doesn't allow us to give up. The secret is to get in touch with the strength of this inner core.

Engrave in your heart and soul the words: 'GIVING UP IS NOT AN OPTION'.

TAKE A SWING AND MAKE IT COUNT

You cannot win by blocking

Defence is good but not good enough in itself to clinch the match for the boxer or the team.

To win you need great offence as well. It feels good to get through a fight without being hit, or at least not too hard, but that will not give you a knockout and/or a win on points.

So bob and weave all you want, show superior footwork, ride or slip the punches, it's all good and well, but to win the battle you will have to do more than that.

Take a swing and make it count

The one thing you can put your money on is that you will at some stage be presented with a gap or a break in life. You may well ask how anyone can be certain of this and the answer is a mathematical one. The law of averages and the science of probability provide proof that nothing remains constant and that there is a very high probability of change in the way events unfold.

The BIG question is: Do you have a trained eye to spot the gap or the break that is there for you to take? Secondly, do you have the guts, the skill and the timing to take a massive swing at that precise time and to make a connection?

If you are afraid you are going to lose the fight or be hit again or you are too tired to move or you have a break in concentration, you may well miss out on the gap or the opportunity that will present itself to you.

When it does, swing, take your best shot at it and make it count. Most of the time one shot at life is all you need to win, to get on top, to do better, to be healed, to save a relationship, to do the right thing.

Make sure your swing counts!

Think twice before you take on an opponent who is above your weight class.

CHALLENGE THOSE WHO DISAGREE WITH YOU

The benefit of a challenge

It is of great benefit to listen to another point of view and anybody who is interested in becoming smarter and learning more absolutely loves to hear an argument opposing their own, especially if the person challenging you is pretty certain about their point of view or their convictions. The more the other person knows about the topic you are debating, the better your chances of gaining insight and sharpening your own point of view for the future.

How not to challenge

There are dumb and smart ways to challenge. If you come across too strong and too arrogant, the other person may do one of two things. He or she may come back equally hard-headed in which case neither party will give or take an inch. This is the most foolish way to go into an argument.

The second thing that may happen is that your opponent will perceive that your ego is prohibiting you from arguing in an adult and constructive way in which case he/she may just walk away from the challenge on the basis that it is just not worth pursuing. In both these cases, you will have won absolutely nothing apart from avoiding a blow to your ego.

The 10% gap

A great negotiator once said that you should always leave a 10% gap in your argument so that you can fill that with some of the sound evidence given by the person you are negotiating or arguing with. It also infers that you are willing to entertain another opinion and, if it's well substantiated, you may accord it a larger percentage, or if it is absolutely solid, you may even consider relinquishing the other 90%. If you refuse to leave the 10% gap you have already made up your mind not to shift your opinion at all, not to learn and not to be convinced, in which case getting into the argument is senseless in the first place.

Stick to the facts

When challenged, it's all too easy to lose sight of the facts and become overly emotional. The reason for this is mostly ego-driven. Remember that the objective is to grow, to learn, to become smarter and to sharpen your tools. Becoming too emotional and attacking the other person on an emotional level is not going to serve you. On the contrary, it is going to detract from your objectives and make you a pitiful negotiator and loser.

Create the 'magic' environment

In the 'magic' environment, both parties can freely express their points of view:

1. They can debate.
2. They can challenge.
3. The can check facts.
4. They can even change their minds.
5. They will feel empowered rather than defeated.
6. They can learn and be thankful.
7. They can move forward with a common understanding, a common vision.

This is the type of environment you want to create when you challenge those who disagree with you. Remember that the objective is to expand your understanding rather than to win at all costs.

BACK YOURSELF BY SHOWING YOUR ART

The proof is in the pudding

The reality TV series *Master Chef* has one component that has viewers glued to their seats ... the moment the contestant puts the dish in front of the judges. At that moment she surrenders all her experience, skill, craft and knowledge so that her 'art' can be judged by the critics.

When the artist who displays his work at the flea market hangs his drawings or paintings and turns the spotlight towards them, he puts forward the skill he brings to his art to you and me – the prospective buyers – to be judged worthy of gracing the walls of our homes or offices or not. At that moment, the artist steps back and becomes vulnerable to the opinion of the public or the judges.

What does it take to show your art?

The obvious word that springs to mind is 'confidence', but if you wait until you declare yourself confident before you put forward your work, by that time you may be an old grey man who no longer cares what the world thinks of him. It takes guts and, as Steven Springfield says in *The War of Art*, you need to overcome the 'resistance' to be able to show your art or level of skill. You can always get better. There will always be another line to draw, an extra ingredient you can add, a final finishing touch, a better backing board for the proposal, another slide you can show, another angle you can cover, etc ... It takes guts to put your work forward to be scrutinised and judged.

It's your turn to show us what you've got

The world is calling on you to show us what you've got. In fact, the world is calling on you every day to put forward your skill, your craft, your mastery, because if you don't we can't buy what you have produced. We cannot hire you. We cannot promote you. We cannot begin to trust you and your work until we become familiar with the quality of your offering, your principles, work ethic and the particular way YOU execute YOUR art.

If you cannot show us your value at work or at the flea market and you fail to overcome the resistance to surrender your art to be judged, you will not survive in the marketplace any longer.

Make the connection

To prosper as an employee in a business or to prosper in your own business, you have to make the connection.

One of my favourite restaurants in Johannesburg must be Tasha's. When you go there at lunchtime, you are allocated a number and have to wait for a table. Yet five steps across the walkway and even right next to Tasha's, will be a restaurant with ample vacant tables while the queue at Tasha's is growing ... Why?

Perhaps you go to a medical centre where there are two doctors with the same qualifications who are equally skilled, but the one has a waiting list, while the other will see you right away ... Why?

At the check-in counter at the airport or while queuing at the bank you may silently wish you'll be served by that one special staff member with whom you have a connection. In fact, you may even allow the person behind you in the queue to be served first because you'd rather wait for that special someone to be free to attend to you.

Another of my favourite restaurants is Turn and Tender. I am prepared to sit inside, outside, wait for a table or call for a booking because I prefer that steakhouse to any other ... Why? For the same reason as the majority of cell phones and airtime are sold in South Africa by PEP, my mentor Brand

Pretorius was voted over and over again the best boss in the country to work for and I drive almost 100 kilometres to take my animals to a veterinarian called Jaco du Plessis.

It's all about the connection. These people and companies put forward their 'art', they show you their authenticity and that's what we want to see and feel. It's because of the connection that we WANT to do business with them.

You have to back yourself, but you have to offer the value, the connection that encourages people to buy your 'art' and admire the way you produce it.

BROADCAST YOURSELF

No need to wait

There is no need to wait for a radio or TV talk show host to call and invite you to be a guest on his or her show.

The strapline of YouTube is 'Broadcast Yourself' – and you can do just that.

It costs nothing to create a YouTube account and you have capability on your smartphone or tab or webcam to make a recording. No more waiting in line to sing your song, to perform your magic or show your cooking skills – say what is on your mind ... we are waiting for you to show us who you are.

What now?

You create a YouTube account or join Instagram or any other platform that may be launched while I'm writing this. You post your videos on your website, on your social media platforms and wherever else you see the opportunity to meaningfully broadcast yourself. If you need to know more about how to do this like a pro, you may want to read the following:

1. 21 Secrets for getting any YouTube video to Rank # 1 by Mick Michaels
2. YouTube Strategies by Paul Colligan
3. Podcast Strategies by Paul Colligan
4. Many others – some are even for free.

By now you should be ready to rock and roll and show the world what it is you have to offer.

Traditional media

If you are lucky and the opportunity presents itself to you, make use of the traditional media. They have their limitations but for some time to come will still appeal to the ordinary man in the street. If you can get onto radio or TV to spread your gospel, you should definitely take the opportunity. You can also always send footage to your contact list or share it on social media or on your website.

Finally

You may well think that the way you make scrambled eggs would be of no value to anyone else. Trust me, if you make mean scrambled eggs or if you can fix a toaster or have a great motivational message, go ahead and broadcast yourself.

Facts are great but learn to trust your gut.

MAINTAIN THE VESSEL

Mens sana in corpore sano

This Latin saying means that a sound mind lives in a healthy body. We all know the holistic connection between mind and body so it is difficult to back yourself when you have neglected your body.

For many intellectuals, hard-working business people, the thinkers of the world, the teachers and others, looking after the body is not always a high priority. It is also a fact that those people (including myself) suffer not only from over-thinking but also over-indulging, which leads to depression and a struggle with the philosophical issues of life. With the help of modern-day medicine, most of you will live until eighty and older. Over that time you do not want to develop a case of 'stinking thinking'. You want to be able to get enough oxygen and nutrients to maintain both a healthy body and mind.

Nutrition and supplements

Due to mass consumption and an ever-growing need for greater production at lower cost, the nutritional value of most foods is degenerating. It is for this reason that we need to consider good supplements to keep both the mind and the body healthy. The body runs on fuel and the quality of the fuel we put into it will generate the quality of the output we get from it.

For us to back ourselves in the future, we will need to research what the 'vessel' will need from a nutritional and supplementation point of view, and ensure that we maintain good health.

Run, Forrest, run!

In the movie *Forrest Gump* his girlfriend would shout, 'Run, Forrest, run' to warn him to escape being bullied. Later in the movie he ran because he had to find a way to release the energy of the mind. Whether you run away, run for, run around, it really doesn't matter and what is more, you can walk if you want. If you do it on a treadmill you don't even have to change your environment. The main thing is to give the body a workout so that the cells can regenerate more easily, the mind can be cleared and opportunities can be envisaged and pursued with an energetic body and a strong mind.

A rude awakening

In the prime of my youth, I sat down for dinner with a young Frenchman.

In the course of general conversation he remarked that one's health is one's wealth. At that time I was both too arrogant and too ignorant to recognise the value of his wise words.

Many years later, in the midst of my wife's chemotherapy, my brother-inlaw, who was visiting us from New Zealand, gave me a rude awakening.

Roy said: 'You say that when Hanlie is better you are going to change your lifestyle, go to gym, eat more healthily ... why THEN, why not RIGHT

NOW? Be the man you are and start by setting an example.'

Your health is your responsibility and your business. No one can look after it for you. If you lose your health, you lose you wealth.

TIME TO TURN PRO

If there is one book you should add to your must-read list, then it is *Turning Pro* by Steven Pressfield. As you begin reading, you get that uneasy feeling which becomes progressively more intense the further you read because there, on almost every page, are described your selfacknowledged weaknesses. Because of these, says the author, you are playing the game of an amateur rather than living the life of a pro.

Pressfield says an amateur is:

1. ego driven
2. easily distracted
3. in search of instant gratification
4. jealous
5. inclined to give his or her power away and live by the opinion of others.

Can you feel how hard-hitting this is? From this you can understand how tempting it is to stay in the amateur league when you doubt that you have enough guts to back yourself and step up to the pro league.

According to Pressfield, some of the traits that characterise a pro are that he or she:

1. reinvents him/herself
2. is patient
3. shows up every day
4. has no excuses
5. says it as it is

6. self-validates.

Having now reflected on Steven Pressfield's list of traits of the amateur vs the pro, you will possibly be inspired to read this and other books by the same author.

A pro backs him/herself

The thing about being an amateur is that you always have the excuse that you don't have to do as well as you could, but if you declare pro status, you are now playing for real. You actually exchange 'playing' for living. There is no more Monopoly money or 'get out of jail free' cards.

The pro has to back him/herself. While an amateur makes a joke about looking forward to the future or laughs about the past, a pro has to be in the now. The games you won or lost in the past and those you may win or lose in the future are devoid of reality; they are mere memories and dreams. Your focus should be on being a pro in the now.

Taking off the headgear

When boxers turn pro, they obtain a professional licence and they remove the protective headgear and the vest. They now fight for the money. A day at the office is spent either at the gym training or in the ring fighting for the money to pay the rent and make a living.

Everything changes when you turn pro. You now need to be as good as you told the world you can be. You now need to prove not to them, but to yourself, that you've got what it takes.

In the process of backing yourself, whether you are working in an office, painting in your studio, arranging flowers or unblocking drains, there will come a time for you to turn pro. When you have gone through this book and done the work, you will be able to turn pro with confidence.

TAKE A DEEP BREATH AND STAY CALM

OMG, it's falling apart

The email was short; it simply requested that I attend a meeting at the CEO's office the next morning. At that stage I had been busy delivering on a contract that I had with this specific company for the past five to six months.

The morning meeting was to inform me that my contract was being cancelled due to the financial pressure the company was under. My first thought was: you can't be serious. The second thought was that I had planned to be there for another six months and had nothing else lined up to fill the time and financial gap the cancellation of this contract would leave in my business.

The overwhelming feeling was: OMG, everything is falling apart!!

Literally days previously I had declined a number of speaking engagements due to this contract. I immediately called the client who had most recently offered me one only to hear that the company would be using the person I had recommended to them in my place. The anxiety intensified at that point. It's falling apart, I thought. This can't be real!

I got to the office and sent an email to one of the companies with whom I had a tender pending only to receive an almost immediate response to the effect that my company had not been successful in the tendering process. So this is it, I thought, an empty pipeline of sales and a cancelled contract by a large company that does not feel anything for a small one-man show like me – YES, it's falling apart!!

Panic

If you ever fall into the deep end and you can't swim, one thing is sure: the sooner you panic, the sooner you will sink to the bottom of the pool.

Panic and fear consume your energy. Worse than that, they freeze your brain, sap your oxygen, tense up your muscles and jeopardise any opportunity you have to survive.

As much as your reptilian brain wants you to go into fight-flight mode, it will not save your business deal – not today, not ever. In a civilised society where the rules are supposed to be fair, you cannot go and break knees or hide in a cave, so face the snakes in suits.

You must not panic – well, at least not show that you are panicking. They will smell it and you will be history.

So what do you do …?

Breathe (again and again)

If you have never tried this, please try it now. It's a better option than to panic.

Give your brain some oxygen, relax your muscles, stay present in the moment and keep breathing. You have just learned the ancient secret of survival, the art practised by masters and gurus alike.

If you back yourself, you will come up with creative ways to solve your crisis within the following few days. Remember, the first objective is simply to get through the moment – the panic attack and the angst that accompany that terrible moment when it feels as if everything is falling apart – and the best way to do that is to breathe.

WHERE IS THE MONEY?

There is no money

This must be one of the most difficult things to grasp because we always associate work with money. At least most of the time, 'Show me the money' – the well-known line from the movie *Jerry Maguire* – would automatically follow the handing over of goods or services.

The question 'Where is the money'? is a paradoxical one. If you follow the suggestions discussed in this book, the money will come. You may not choose to believe this and argue that only if you know there is money will you make the effort to follow them. The choice is yours.

Give it a go and you will see that your love for and knowledge of what you do, plus the passion and tenacity you bring to the work you do, will produce what you need. So perhaps a chapter about trust should have been included here, just for the sceptics.

What is money?

Money is the currency in which energy is rewarded. This may sound quite metaphysical but it's true. For the effort, skill and energy you put into your work, you deserve a payslip at the end of the month. If you stop at the car wash and the rollers of the machine clean your car and the dryers dry it, you pay for that service. If you buy food to enjoy and to nourish yourself, you pay money for that. The concept is simple: energy equals a reward.

If you are putting in an extra effort, doing your job with love and showing your skill and craft to the world, should you receive more money? Well, here is how it works. If you bring passion and skill to your work, you will firstly derive more pleasure from what you do, and that will cascade into adding more value, delivering better energy and getting paid more. Having said that, remember that you determine your own value.

When you accept the job or the contract you have agreed on with your employer, the monetary value needs to be paid to you for your input.

The great magnifier

The most amazing thing about power is that money has the ability to magnify it. So if you are a good person with good intentions and a valuedriven attitude who cares about people and appreciates life, money will magnify that. If you are a super-jerk who uses and abuses people and are self-centred with little love for your fellow man, money will magnify that too. Isn't it poetic justice how the attitude and mindset that determines what you get for your effort and how you obtain it tends to magnify who you really are?

Stuff the expenses – up the income (or maybe not)

When you are confident about your ability to sell, this positive attitude will serve you well. However, any financial advisor will tell you it is as important to keep expenses under control.

A sensible approach will be:

1. Work hard to create a good pipeline of sales and strive to maintain a high closing ratio.
2. Keep expenses under control and have a lean mindset when it comes to spending money.

3. Build up some reserves to fall back on and give you some peace of mind.

It's your money. Make it work for you.

BEYOND THE '-ISMS'

What is an '-ism'?

In the context it is used here, an '-ism' is an ideology expressing a belief in the superiority of a certain class. So it's a type of doctrine of which examples are racism, sexism, classism and even scepticism. Now you see where all this is going and why we would need to go beyond these social '-isms' if we want to be successful and significant in the world in which we operate and live.

Why go beyond the 'isms'?

You just have to speak to my friend Jenna Clifford to hear why we should have moved beyond some of these '-isms' a long time ago. Of course not all '-isms' are negative but when it comes to a belief system that includes certain people and labels others in order to keep them on the fringes of society and business, we should definitely do our best to eradicate it.

One of Jenna Clifford's pet subjects is to bring awareness to the harmful impact that sexism has on woman and on the economy of any country.

For example, according to the Bangladeshi economist, Dr Muhammad Yunus, in India a dollar in the hand of a woman goes ten times further than in the hand of a man because women are by nature less selfish and put the needs of the family before their own. So sexism in business and other spheres is one of those things we must work hard to eradicate, not only from the world but from our vocabulary.

In a world where people are labelled and judged because of their gender, their class, their sexual orientation or their religion, it becomes increasingly difficult for these people to back themselves.

The responsibility lies with all of us to make these negative social '-isms' disappear.

If you are going to take a swing at someone or something, make it count.

MONDAY AT ABOUT 4:25 PM

Everybody's Free (to wear sunscreen) by Baz Luhrmann

'... The real troubles in your life are apt to be the things that never crossed your worried mind, the kind that blindside you at 4 pm on some idle Tuesday.'

This song came out in 1999 and little did I know then how true these words would prove to be in my own life and how I would quote them in this book. There are all sorts of statistics regarding worry. Some say 40% of the things you worry about happen and you can do nothing about it.

Another 40% will never happen. 12% of worries are needless worries about health and miscellaneous issues. 8% are real of which 4% you can do something about and 4% you can do nothing about. The sunscreen song says the same thing, just in a different way. No real need to worry because you really don't know what the hell is waiting for you in the future.

Monday, 4:25 pm

In the song Luhrmann mentions an idle Tuesday at 4 pm. In my life it happened on a Monday at about 4:25 pm when the surgeon told my perfectly healthy wife, who thought she had some indigestion, that she has cancer and that it is serious. All the studying I have done, all the books I have read and all the bad news I have heard in my life couldn't have prepared me for that moment. There are many analogies

I can give you – that it took my breath away, that I felt my knees giving way, that my heart was pounding in my chest, that I vomited, etc but you will not understand or know what I am talking about until your 'Monday' comes.

The reason I am sharing this very personal story with you is that a week later, when I wrote this piece, I realised that a day will come in all of our lives when all we know may not be enough. That day will call for you to truly back yourself. There will be moments when you won't be able to see how you will ever get through it. You may well need the love and support of friends and family which will strengthen you, but in essence it is your event, the beginning of a journey you will have to walk step by step.

There will be people – magic people – to hold your hand, encourage you, spur you on ... but it will still be your event, your journey. When you close your eyes at night, your friends and family may have said their prayers for you and you may have said yours, but then you are there by yourself. It is at these times that you will hopefully have grown enough backbone to back yourself.

You will have to bite harder on the gum guard and know that it is your fight. A word of advice – this is no time to doubt what you know or ponder whether you have done enough to get through this. This is a time of faith. It is a time to have hope for the future, to give it everything you have, and to back yourself no matter what.

No one knows whether this will be enough, but you will have no other choice and my intuition tells me it will go along way towards getting you through whatever your 'Monday' challenge is. It may or may not work out the way you want it to, but you will get through it if you choose to back yourself.

GETTING PAST 'NO' AND MAYBE' TO 'YES'

Your value propositions

If you have something of value to offer, you will not have to negotiate much, and perhaps not even at all.

If you are selling and you have a good product or service and you can show the prospective buyer the value and why they should buy the product/service from you, there will be no need to hear the words 'no' or 'maybe'. What you will hear is 'yes!'

How do we do it? We all know certain things are easier to sell than others, but if you do your homework, you will have an easier time making a deal. To sell fresh air is difficult, but to sell it to someone under water or down in a mine where there is no fresh air is literally a breeze.

Part of making a sale and getting what you want is to do your prospecting well and to qualify your potential client. For example, if my cell phone company calls me offering a free phone and a great package, even though I am already a client and have just received a new handset and I'm already on the top package, I may just try and sell them a sales programme on how to qualify a buyer.

Back yourself by making your value proposition as attractive as possible to the right client and you will never have to enter into a potential horsetrading situation.

Anticipate

In the great TV series *Suits*, the leading character, a man by the name of

Harvey Specter, is all about anticipation. His strength is to know before the others know, to anticipate a move before it's made and to anticipate a thought before it's spoken.

When in negotiations, this unseen power of anticipation can give you the edge. It has a little of two ingredients in it – anticipation, which is a

gut feeling or intuition, mixed with experience.

If you can anticipate the objections a person may raise, you can

brainstorm good arguments beforehand to counteract these. Just

imagine walking into your boss's office to ask for an increase in salary,

having thought through all the possible objections he/she could come

up with, and you have a great reply for each of them. This will put you in

such a powerful position.

Know when to walk away

In his song *The Gambler*, Kenny Rogers sings: *'You got to know when to*

hold them, know when to fold them, know when to walk away and know

when to run.'

There is a point during some negotiations when you realise that your strategy isn't working and you decide to walk away. To walk away is not a sign of weakness; on the contrary, it is a sign of strength.

The key to negotiating successfully is to curb your emotions, think clearly and rationally, look at the different options, put yourself in the other person's shoes, argue the issue from both sides, fall back on your experience, and use your gut. By doing this you should be able to come up with more solutions than problems, but should it become clear that you are getting nowhere, despite your best efforts, it's time to walk away.

THE VALUE OF A HANDSHAKE

What does a handshake mean?

As far back as the 5th Century BC handshakes were used by the ancient Greeks. A generally accepted definition of a handshake is that it is a brief interlocking of two people's hands, usually accompanied by a short inward or downward motion. Furthermore, it can be seen as a peace offering or to conclude some agreement reached. Legend has it that when the hand has no weapon in it and it is used to shake another person's hand, it is a sign of reconciliation.

Nelson Mandela's memorial service

In December 2013 South Africa and the world at large lost a phenomenal and charismatic leader – Nelson Mandela. He died at the age of 95.

He must be the latest of the big transformational leaders who have passed on and definitely the man who gained the most respect in the world for peaceful transformation.

At his memorial service in Soweto, world leaders gathered to honour him and to pay their final respects. The dignitaries were from all over the world, not only from different countries, but also from different ideologies. During this ceremony a single handshake caught the attention of the world media. President Barak Obama without any hesitation shook the hand of Raul Castro, brother of the Cuban leader

Fidel Castro. The media showed the clip of the handshake over and over.

Moments later social media sites were buzzing with what it really meant and the significance of the handshake.

For me it was just another sign of the power of Nelson Mandela to bring together those who think they are separated from one another by their differing ideologies, a demonstration to the world 'from the grave' that in essence we are all human beings plotting our way the best we see fit here on the blue planet.

Your handshake

For years to come you will greet many with a handshake and say farewell to as many with the same handshake. You will conclude deals and use the handshake as a gesture of agreement. You may even walk away from a deal or a relationship with a handshake to demonstrate there are no hard feelings.

You can also take the decision to 'load' your handshake with intention, meaning that when you extend the gesture to someone, you put something of your essence, your energy and your soul into it. In this way you leave the other person with a bit of yourself. When they turn around and walk away they take with them a speck of your energy, your attention, your love, your compassion and your significance.

Wouldn't it be wonderful to send off both friend and foe with a handshake and some positive energy to remember you by?

LEADERS WHO BACK THEMSELVES AND THEIR PEOPLE, AND THOSE WHO DON'T

Definition of leadership

There must be millions of definitions of this very important topic. While researching it I came across good ones, specific ones and not-so-good ones. The reason it is so difficult to define is that there are so many aspects of leadership. For instance there are:

1. types of leadership
2. specific qualities that characterise leaders
3. styles of leadership
4. industry requirements
5. environmental factors ... and many more.

With all of these complexities present, perhaps one should resort to simplicity: Leadership is 'the ability to give direction and get people to follow.' This works for me now.

Cotton balls, jaw-breaker balls, sour balls and brass balls

If you have ever driven past a field of cotton balls you will know that it's so out of the ordinary that you almost have to stop and look. The thing about cotton balls is that their beauty contrasts so starkly with the dry and dull environment in which they grow. It's almost as if one doesn't expect to see them there.

A leader needs that soft side, that unexpected beauty and gentleness in a rugged environment, that ability to care and deal with the soft issues. Cotton balls can also rot and perish. For a leader to always act like a cotton ball will never work as there will come times when it's necessary

to put the beauty and softness aside.

Then there is the hard sweet some of us grew up with is often called a jaw-breaker ball. As its name suggests, this sweet-tasting boiled sweet is impossible to break with one bite, and can damage your teeth if you're not careful. The colouring in the sweet also turns your tongue black.

Sometimes a leader needs to be hard and leave his or her stain on a situation. One can do this in a nice way but the downside to being simultaneously sweet and hard is the risk of being seen as not quite genuine and you don't want to be suspected of being a fake when you lead people.

The sour ball is also a sweet that has a hard texture but has a sour taste.

Some people may like it but in this parable I am using the sour ball to represent the antagonist.

Sour balls are hard, sour and stain your mouth. A leader who is consistently hard leaves his/her mark but with a sour taste in the mouth, will never be respected and will create an environment of mistrust and disrespect.

The brass balls represent a willingness to go where no one else has gone before, to be able to face uncertainty and back yourself. They imply a courageous nature that does not crumble in the face of adversity or difficulties, and strives to make a difference no matter what it takes.

We have all seen and experienced those leaders who appear to be all fired up to make a difference, to transform the company, to get individuals to express their greatness, and then we find out that they are only in it for themselves. They back off when the heat is on. We see them go back on their word, negate their responsibility and become soft like cotton, hard like jaw-breaker balls, make us feel nauseous like sour balls, and appear lack-lustre when compared to the attributes of brass balls.

We have also seen the opposite – those leaders who give people the opportunity to live meaningful lives, who makes a difference, who are soft when life requires them to show heart, who can be firm like a jaw-breaker ball when it is required, who will not give in to negativity or anything sour at all, and who will show courage and live the ethos of those brass-ball warriors.

The culture

Leadership determines culture and if you think it doesn't, you are wrong.

Every company has a way of doing things, benchmarks of behaviour – an unspoken culture. This way of doing things and the mindset behind it is determined by the leadership of the company.

There is a company in Africa, known to most Africans I would suspect, called PEP Stores. PEP is a discount clothing company that has diversified into home ware, foot ware and cell phones to name a few. They purposefully drive a culture and, if I were to share the actions that drive this culture with you, you would either want to apply for a job at PEP right away or hurry off to buy their products. Daily, specific behaviours are demonstrated by leadership and annually employees attend conventions which are held countrywide. These present the opportunity to imbed the culture and the zest for the brand, as well as to show the staff how much they are appreciated.

I once heard that culture or values are the things people do even if no one is watching. This behaviour is shaped and patterned by extraordinary leadership that allows people to make a difference.

No one can make you feel inferior without your consent. Eleanor Roosevelt

THE CORPORATE STORY

Thinking about the corporate world, there are many true stories of people who started off in the mailing room, or as a teller in a bank, or as a welder on a plant and, by applying a set of principles, later got to the top of the organisation. Even more wonderful is the fact that many of these people came from not very affluent households. They therefore didn't have the luxury of an influential contact or family member to push them to the front of the line, so to speak, and thereby kick-start their career growth. These people started work, found that they enjoyed the industry and decided that this was the right career for them. They studied part time, did every internal course they could, put their hands up whenever there was an opportunity, and sometimes got picked and sometimes not. In short, they stuck at it and their tenacity eventually paid off.

I deliberately chose not to tell a story of someone I know personally because there are truly just too many. I would however like to share with you a story of attitude. Two days after my dad's funeral I had to report his death to the executors of his estate so that they could start the process of winding it up. I called the bank that had been appointed to act as executor and got through to a lady by the name of Ronelle.

I introduced myself and the first thing she did was to express her condolences on the death of my father and the hope that the family would find comfort in their grief.

She explained that there was a list of about 35 things to be handed in and taken care of to start the process. She then said: 'I know this is a terrible time for you and that the last thing on your mind right now is some

119

administrative process. I am going to help you with this. If we can get the first five items done we can get going.' A day or two later, that's exactly what happened. She helped us with every single thing, kept us in the loop and made sure we were comfortable with the progress. She did an amazing job. She didn't have to but she did it because she cared and because she thrived on being good at doing what she had chosen to do.

Soon after she dealt with us Ronelle was offered a much better job in a more senior position. She got it because of the way she chose to apply her knowledge and skill and because she cares about the people she works with. Here is a person who backs herself with every task she carries out and every client she comes into contact with.

You don't have to work for yourself or be an artist or a poet to create art or poetry. You can do that in any corporate position. You may think that the organisation is not paying enough attention to what you do and how you do it and you may well be right. Remember, you are actually doing it for yourself. It is your art and your poetry. Do not allow a system or a procedure or a performance appraisal to influence you. Do it with passion and create significance for yourself.

At the height of laughter, the universe is flung into a kaleidoscope of new possibilities. JOan Houston

THE STORY OF BELLA

Let me share with you the story of Bella. She is the youngest of three children born to a mother and father who lived on a farm in the far north of North West Province. Her soft-hearted nature and easy-going ways endeared her to her family and those around her.

On weekend mornings, as a young girl, you would find her standing on a box preparing breakfast for the family on a non-electric, non-gas stove fuelled with wood. She knew how to get the hob plates to just the right temperature so that her breakfast and crumpets would come out perfectly. In later years at school she excelled in home industry studies, but it was never an option for her to attend a culinary college to study to become a chef or to work in any other food-related industry. Instead

Bella studied education and qualified as a pre-primary school teacher.

Her love for cooking and baking remained a passion and at dinner parties and birthdays there was never any shortage of compliments for her baking and cooking. Life happened and took a few turns, as it does with all of us. In her early thirties the opportunity to get involved in the restaurant business finally presented itself and, to everyone's surprise, she absolutely hated it. She resigned and out of sheer desperation started a small home bakery business supplying cakes and biscuits to a few delis and restaurants.

Bella's library of books grew and her friends and family knew that at Christmas, on her birthday or on any other special occasion a cook book would always be welcome. She began to read and study trends on the internet and became a follower of blogs of many of the famous and notso-famous chefs and food writers.

Then she spotted a gap in the market. More and more people were looking for wheat- and gluten-free products ... Bella had a new interest.

She read everything she could lay her hands on about the subject and bought gluten-free flour from small and obscure shops that import it from Ethiopia and several other places. She used this in her baking but most of her initial experiments failed. The products tasted like cardboard, only a little softer.

Bella knew that gluten-free would be the next big thing, so she persevered until eventually one or two of the products became edible.

She then began to offer these products to her existing small network of delis and restaurants.

She was never a person who enjoyed the limelight and had a phobia of public speaking, so when the request from a large health store came to address their delegates at a conference on the value of glutenfree products, she froze up and declined. Thankfully, the lady who organised the event pushed harder and promised to be on stage with her. Bella obliged and, medicated with tranquillisers, she did a brilliant presentation. Her products were flying off the shelves. Soon after this, she shared the stage with health food gurus such as Patrick Holford and others.

She then received an invitation to meet with possibly the biggest wholesale health food distributors in South Africa. They offered her a job but she declined. They upped the offer and she declined again. They then said, 'If we buy your business you can come and do what you love for us and we will not only pay you a salary, but also commission on the sale of all your products.' She accepted.

Bella is still today the 'go to' person when it comes to wheat-free and gluten-free baking in South Africa. The products she developed are sold in health stores and by large pharmacy groups. Bella is living her dream.

If you read this true story and get it, but really get it, you will know exactly what to do in order to live your dream.

GIVING AND RECEIVING REQUIRE OPEN HANDS

Open your hands

Mother Teresa once said that the biggest advantage goes to the giver, not to the receiver. It's interesting to note that both giving and receiving require your hands to be open. Whether the blessing goes to the one who gives or the one who receives is definitely debatable. In your life you will hopefully experience both.

For you to experience the fullness of life, you will have to gracefully practise both giving and receiving. It starts with being 'open'. Once you open your hands to either give or receive the mind follows suit and universal truths such as reciprocating, attraction, gratitude and significance become evident.

In business you will very seldom hear about these principles of kindness, attraction, personal significance and others, mostly because business is seen as 'war'.

Statements such as:

1. It's a war out there
2. Fight for market share

We defeated the competition ... are often associated with business but when you look more closely you find real people with kind hearts and good intentions doing the best they can to earn an honest living.

There is nothing wrong with being competitive and you have to be if you want to maintain longevity in any kind of market. Having said that, perhaps a slightly different approach and a more open-hearted and open-handed mindset will lessen the stress, heart attacks and all other physical and mental disorders that plague our work environments.

Giving

Backing yourself also means being there for others. You may think you don't have much to offer, but you are wrong.

All individuals have value for all other individuals. This is the law of oneness. Neale Donald Walsch once made a statement that became the credo for my own life when he said, 'In the absence of that which I am not, that which I am cannot exist.' This means that I am because of you and when I give to you or anyone else I give to myself. The contribution we make to one is a contribution to us all.

Your knowledge, your skills, your love and all you do and how you do it will be a contribution to us all.

By backing yourself you will give hope to others to do the same.

Receiving

Maybe Suze Orman has it right when she says that you nett worth equals your self-worth. To be able to receive you will have to keep your hands and heart open, and consider yourself worthy enough to receive abundantly. You cannot expect others to value you more highly than you value yourself.

It is often at the most unlikely times in life that some friend, family member or even a stranger will step up to back you. At these times the best you can do is to accept their generosity gracefully and acknowledge that you are worthy of being backed.

Recently, at the most unlikely time, a client and friend, Meyer Benjamin, stepped up and offered me a car for my private use when we really needed an extra car for a few months. It is at times like these that if ever you doubted the kindness of the human spirit you would have to concede that it is alive and well and truly makes the world a better place.

Relationships

Whether you give or receive you will always stand in relation to something or someone else. If you receive oxygen from plants, for example, you are in some relationship with nature.

Life is about relationships. In your relationship with yourself, other people, nature, all things and God, you can only exist in relation to something else. The kinder you are to yourself and all others, the better your chances are of being able to back yourself, be backed by others and back others.

The Libyan poet Kahlil Gibran said, 'You have helped me in my work and in myself. And I have helped you in your work and in yourself. And I am grateful to heaven for this you-and-me.'

I know you're tired but come, this is the way.
Rumi

LET'S GO DEEPER – SEEDING YOUR CONSCIOUSNESS

Would going deeper help?

At the outset, this book was not intended to go really deep at all. The intention was to give some very practical suggestions to make yourself marketable and to give a definite edge to the already pretty sharp guys and girls out there. A lot of contemplation went into the decision to put this piece in the book. The tipping point was a flashback to the one book that changed my life at a very young age.

The book *Illusions* written by Richard Bach came to me when I most needed it and gave me hope that there must be more to life than my seemingly mediocre experience in a small town in the North West Province.

If you haven't read *Illusions* yet, make a plan to read it, possibly in conjunction with *Handbook of the Reluctant Messiah*. In this way you will see the value of going deeper, becoming more conscious and creating a deeper connection with yourself and all other things in our universe.

Seeding your consciousness

'Just remember in the winter far beneath the bitter snow, lies the seed that with

the sun's love in the spring becomes the rose' (Bette Midler – The Rose).

As we go through life we learn. At the time of the learning we may not see the value of the lessons or the information we receive. We read books, we go through experiences, we speak to friends, we observe and then one day we find we need to fall back on the knowledge, on the experience, and the seed sprouts to serve us.

We don't know when we will need the learning we have gone through, but none if it is ever in vain. When we come to know this we can then purposefully set out to learn more, understand more deeply, connect more genuinely and make sure we collect those seeds that will, with the sun's rays, blossom.

Learning can take place on a number of different levels – ranging from a physical or platonic level to a mental, emotional or spiritual level.

As our awareness expands and our need to get more from life than a platonic experience becomes more urgent, so we grow in consciousness.

We make deeper connections with the events, things and people in our lives. We are actively seeding our consciousness to get more from life, to derive meaning and significance through all we experience.

Should we go deeper? A personal question that can only be answered by you.

How will you find the answer? If you wish to find an answer, you will only find it by going deeper.

All those great secrets of success won't work unless you do.

THE ROAD TO SHAMBHALA

Where is it?

Wash away my troubles, wash away my pain with the rain in Shambhala.

Wash away my sorrow, wash away my shame with the rain in Shambhala.

These are the opening lines of the song *Shambhala* by Three Dog Night, 1975.

According to Wikipedia, Shambhala is an Indian/Buddist mythical kingdom. We would all love to get to or experience such a place where all is good and well – a Nirvana, a Heaven, a Promised Land if you will.

Naturally, we all wish we could follow a map to find Shambhala, but even though that's not possible I may just have some directions for you.

At this point you're probably wondering why I would include directions to 'Shambhala' in a book titled *Back Yourself*. The answer is that sooner rather than later you will need to find a place to rejuvenate, to recharge your energy and re-activate your creativity. While you are on the go doing what you love, making a difference and living your life to the fullest, it would probably never cross your mind that you may at some stage need directions to Shambhala.

Yet the time will come when you will be Googling directions, looking for a road map, considering a new diet, joining a meditation class, finding your way to a holy place to experience one of the most sought-after states in human consciousness called peace.

In the book *The Road Less Travelled*, M Scott Peck says that this road is the road to the self. You may Google it or find a guru, master or leader to learn from, but the directions I am going to share with you now may just help you find what you are looking for:

1. The journey is within – not without.
2. Other people can tell you about how they found their special place of peace, but you must find your own.
3. If you embark on this journey with fear you will never find it.
4. If you embark on it with love, you are almost there.
5. The journey is as important as the destination.
6. When you get there you will know that the welcoming party will be you welcoming yourself.

At the 'place', at the core of your inner self, you will find peace and strength to motivate you to cope with life and death, and to revitalise you so that you can back yourself.

But it's been no bed of roses

no pleasure cruise

I consider it a

challenge before the

whole human race

And I ain't gonna lose.

Queen: We are the champions